A Mother's
Right To Cry

A Mother's Right To Cry

Alice McLaughlin

iUniverse, Inc.
Bloomington

A MOTHER'S RIGHT TO CRY

iUniverse books may be ordered through booksellers or by contacting:

iUniverse
1663 Liberty Drive
Bloomington, IN 47403
www.iuniverse.com
1-800-Authors (1-800-288-4677)

Because of the dynamic nature of the Internet, any web addresses or links contained in this book may have changed since publication and may no longer be valid. The views expressed in this work are solely those of the author and do not necessarily reflect the views of the publisher, and the publisher hereby disclaims any responsibility for them.

Any people depicted in stock imagery provided by Thinkstock are models, and such images are being used for illustrative purposes only.
Certain stock imagery © Thinkstock.

ISBN: 978-1-4759-7657-1 (sc)
ISBN: 978-1-4759-7658-8 (ebk)

Printed in the United States of America

iUniverse rev. date: 03/09/2013

Contents

This Mother's Journey

This book came out of the journey of meeting fear and grief's unrelenting force.

In these heartbreaking happenings within this walk through life, I would never have made it if it had not been for the strong core belief that God was escorting me through these valleys. When He talks about walking through the valley, He does not intend for us to go through these times alone.

Throughout this book, there is one example after another of His presence in each instance, guiding, comforting, and encouraging, either by impression or the touch of a friend. The belief and understanding of His written word, the Bible, gives unlimited grace and peace while enduring tough times. For many years, He has been an integral part of our life, and during this time, people were used in many instances to uplift, encourage, and pray when it was just too hard to do it alone.

A Mother's Right to Cry reveals how precious our loved ones are and how fragile life is.

Then the subtle movement of God begins to bring forth the unexplainable sense of inner peace.

This book is written to encourage all who have faced crisis and trauma. We just don't know when trouble will come knocking on our door. It appears that life is good, or at least nothing is going on that we can't handle. Then one day or night, we get a phone call, and our life goes from peaceful to unbelievable pain. When this happens and we can't think, breath, or grasp what is happening, we need someone or something to turn to. This is when God, in His infinite mercy, shows up in the form of friends and loved ones to help us make it through the next minutes, hours, days, and weeks.

When your crisis has culminated, and you are trying to put your life back together into some sense of normalcy, I hope this book will help you see that God has been with you through it all, giving you the strength that you didn't know you had. When the storms of life hit, they often hit hard. I've found that in the painful beatings of the fear of the unknown, terror, stress and confusion, He brought that peace that passes all understanding, and the stronghold of joy that got me through it all. That is why people thought I was trying to be Superwoman when I was fighting to stay sane. I felt like a swimmer trying to stay afloat while the waves of crisis were pulling me down. Yet my God, my heavenly Father, was my life raft.

Rex, a friend of mine, who is a pastor at the church I attend, writes and records music. He had a bad dream one night and when he woke up, the Lord, in His still quiet voice began to reassure Rex with the words of this song, "Walking' on the Streets of Gold." His wife died several years ago, and he believes she is in heaven. The dream was so bad that it shook Rex to the core. With the writing of this song, he became calm and assured that his wife really is in heaven, "dancing' on the streets of gold."

When I speak of the Lord speaking to Rex, it is words that came into Rex's mind as thoughts inspired by his love and belief in God.

I asked him if I could put the chorus of his song in this book, and he agreed. He recorded this song and two others to share with the readers of this book.

My prayer and hope is that as you read this book and realize God's presence throughout it that you will want to hear the recordings as well.

The address below is available for you to request your copy of this awesome recording.

BakerSongs@Yahoo.com

A Mother's Right to Cry

ames was born with the umbilical cord wrapped around his neck three times and his body bruised from the lack of oxygen. From the beginning, James faced life's adversities.

When he was three years old, James nearly died. We were living in Thunder Mountain, a dry, dusty town in the California desert. A new copper mine was being developed, and Don, James' father, was part of the construction crew. We lived in a manufactured home in a trailer park, where most of the other families lived because of this new mine site.

One of the crew members came over to our house so Don could help him work on the engine of his pickup. It was early evening when the guys went out to start working; of course, our three-year-old son had to go out and "help" also.

The evening wore on, and as it began to grow dark, I knew Don and James would be coming in soon. I heard the pickup engine start to rumble and knew it would not be long.

Suddenly, I had this urging within to go out and find James. I pushed the thought away, firmly believing James would come in with his father. The urging became more insistent and finally, I relented and went outside. As I walked down the steps from the house, I saw what looked like a pile of rags under the passenger side of the pickup. I walked around the pickup to where Don was standing and asked him where James was. He looked surprised, as he'd thought James was in the house.

Scanning the area as I walked back to the passenger side of the pickup, I stooped over and looked under the pickup. There on the ground was not a pile of rags but our son, fast asleep. The pickup was positioned in such a way that it would have crushed James when it started moving. Don and his friend were horrified. That night they didn't get much sleep, because they couldn't shake the terrible thoughts of what almost happened. If I had not listened to that insistent, urgent voice, our son would have died that night. I did sleep peacefully because tragedy had been averted.

"Give unto the Lord the glory due to His name" (Psalm 29:2a).

James' early childhood was one deeply fraught with disappointment and pain.

When he was four, his father and I divorced, which devastated him. We have no idea what divorce does to our children. James would cry and stomp his feet and scream, "Why did you leave my daddy?" Tears coursed down his face, and the anger and despair that poured out of his devastation broke my heart. There was nothing I could say that would repair what had been done. The pain drove him into the arms of trouble. He also had an older sister, who was five years old and a younger brother who was three years old, who were equally affected by the divorce.

When I remarried, there were four stepsisters and a stepfather to contend with, and life became harder. This meant he had four sisters in addition to his own sister and younger brother. I am sure he was a frightened, overwhelmed little boy with so much to deal with. James and his sister lived with us for a year and a half, and then he went to live with his father and younger brother who had stayed with his dad. Even coming to stay with us in the summer became very difficult for him. We were a dysfunctional family, and every one of the children were miserable. Each one acted out in different ways and ended up in trouble. Using illegal drugs, stealing, rebellion, running away, and ending up in juvenile court were their ways of acting out their feelings and pain.

Every one of those children experienced the same emotions James was feeling and acted out in various ways. Each one was a very troubled child, and no one knew how to help them sort out the feelings and fears of the devastation of divorce. We did not have the resources that are available today for adults and children to help deal with those emotions. However, even with help, children of divorce still experience these same emotions.

My stepchildren were older, and the oldest one became involved in drugs and rebellious behavior. As time moved forward, she introduced her sisters, stepsister, and brother into the drug world. These years were the Age of Aquarius—the years of the hippie movement, living in communes, smoking marijuana, and taking LSD and other mind-altering drugs.

A short time after I married my second husband, we moved to Canyon City, Texas. This was a college town, high in the mountains of Texas. This place introduced the downfall of these children.

Canyon City is located in a beautiful area, with lots of outdoor activities to pursue.

It is a wonderful place to live if you like fishing, hunting, hiking, and skiing or just enjoying a fun camping trip to get closer to nature. We often took the kids to the hills to picnic and camp. We saw lots of wildlife. A deer even came into our camp one evening until the kids couldn't stay still any longer, and the startled animal bounded off into the woods. We often saw herds of elk and deer from the car as we were driving on mountain roads. The streams were wild and beautiful with the background of so many different trees and bushes. It was a place to relax and enjoy God's creation. Those were good times and good memories.

Then we moved back to California. By this time, two of the oldest stepdaughters had moved to Texas to live with their mother. My oldest daughter and James had been living with their father in Carlin, California, but James, who was now 12 years old, was getting into trouble, and we thought he might do better living with me. I wasn't working outside the home, and we thought the stability of a parent being home full time might help.

I wish I could say that it made the difference. Unfortunately, it got worse. He was back in the environment with stepsisters, as well as with a stepfather who didn't deal well with troubled children—his own or someone else's. James became very troubled and in trouble, getting into fights, stealing (which I learned much later), destroying other people's property, and more.

James had grown up to be quite a handsome young man. He had shoulder-length dark blond hair, blue eyes, and was just a couple inches short of six feet tall. His face had a light sprinkling of freckles and a ready smile—or frowns of anger.

James, the Armed Robber

Empty Guns and Wrong Motives

As he grew older, James got into more and more trouble, each event worse than the one before. I vividly recall one day when the juvenile officer called to tell me James had been jailed for armed robbery. I nearly fainted. The officer said that the gun was not loaded, but the lady at who James had pointed the gun did not know that, and she was scared to death. I could not believe he would do such a violent thing.

James had to go before the judge, and James was sent to the reform school for delinquent boys for six months.

James turned seventeen on April 26, 1980, the day he was released from reform school. He did very well at first—he got a job, and everything seemed okay. It wasn't long, however, before he lost his job. He began staying out late, coming home drunk, and got involved in fights and doing drugs. He brought home an orange-colored glass bong (it stood three feet high!), used for smoking marijuana. The bottom part of the bong held water, and the top held the marijuana and had a tube with a mouth piece. It looked like something out of *The Arabian Nights*.

Furiously, I screamed at him to get out of my house and take that thing with him. I know my face was red, my eyes were shooting darts, and I wanted to hit him!

I called James' probation officer, Mr. Clarence, and demanded that James be arrested and put back in reform school. He found James and arrested him. He was going to incarcerate him for a few days to try to get him straightened out. When they got to the jail, James jumped out of the vehicle and ran. He jumped into a railroad boxcar and fled all the way to California. He changed his mind, however, and came back. He wanted to make arrangements with me and Mr. Clarence to actively seek employment. He said if he did not get a job, he would go to reform school without resistance.

In retrospect, his getting a job wasn't the issue. The drinking, using drugs, and disobeying the law were the issues. Getting a job just made these things more accessible. One night he came home in a drunken rage. He stood outside in his underwear, beating on my pickup with his fists, and screaming at God. I don't know why he was doing that, except he was so unhappy and angry at life.

James found a job with a seismograph crew the next day, drilling for mineral and ore samples. He worked for a month and things went smoothly at first. James earned good wages with this job, which meant more to spend on drugs and alcohol. Soon, James was again without a job. He assured me this was temporary. I knew James was deeply troubled, and I began praying as I never had before. Although I had no idea at the time, God was preparing me for upcoming sorrows.

During our Wednesday night services, my pastor preached a series of sermons titled "God's Grace Is Sufficient." The message was that God's grace encompasses all situations. Those sermons seemed like a pipeline between the pastor and me. I absorbed every word.

Terrifying Moments and Broken Lives

ames's aunt and uncle came up from California to visit his grandmother, who lived in Carlin, California. James said he was going to see them, and I encouraged him to go. His father, sister, and brother lived there also, so it would be a fun time.

The day after James left, a young man stopped by my house seeking James. He said that his sister had not come home for several days, and he had heard James had been with her. I told him my son was in Carlin, visiting family.

The following day, James' sister, Maryann, called and said that James had been to Carlin but he had left. He told her he was in some kind of trouble but didn't give her any details.

On Saturday afternoon, I sat in the beauty shop getting a permanent. I was halfway done when someone brought in a newspaper for that day. The front page headlines mentioned a girl named Jena, the sister of the young man who had come to my house on Thursday. Her badly decomposed body had been found by two joggers, in the desert, southwest of town. I knew the authorities would consider James to be a person of interest and would be searching for him. I sat in that chair, not saying a word, but screaming on the inside.

After paying the hair stylist, I ran for my pickup and headed out to Creek Side, where James' friend lived. I thought he might know where James was. On the way, my pickup engine quit running. I decided to walk, but after a few hundred yards in the in the blazing California heat, I was grateful when a young man on a motorcycle offered to give me a ride to my friends home. It wasn't until after the young man rode away that I discovered no one was home. It was several miles out in the country, and my ride was gone. I was left to contemplate walking to the next ranch. Just then, James' father arrived with our other two children in his pickup.

"Do you know where James is?" he asked. "Did you hear the news?"

"Yes, I've heard, but I haven't seen him since he left to visit everyone in Carlin." I then climbed into my ex-husband's truck and slammed the heavy door!

As we approached my broken-down pickup, we saw that James' friend Jay and his dad had stopped to see if I needed help. I slid out of the pickup and ran across the road to Jay. "Do you know where James could be?" I asked. "Have you heard he is in trouble?" Jay said he hadn't heard, nor did he have any idea where James had gone. He was lying, but I didn't know that then.

Just then, the police drove up and approached Don and me. Once they determined who we were, they asked to speak with us in town at my home. They also told me they were impounding my pickup.

The police arrived at my home shortly after Don and I did. They began asking questions related to Jena's death. They wanted to know about a shovel that had been found at the scene. Did it look like the one that had been in the back of my pickup, they wanted to know, and was it mine?

It looked like the shovel that had been in my pickup but the same type of shovels look alike. The shovel found at the scene had been out in the sun and weather for over a week, so it was rusty; mine had not been rusty the last time I saw it.

All the questions were frustrating, because we couldn't tell them anything. They told us to go to the police station and sign a statement. I didn't know until much later that we should have requested an attorney before we answered any questions. We did as we were told and then returned to my house to wait—and to see if James would call. Don decided to go home, so he could be there if James should call him. He also needed to take our other two children home. They were tired and afraid.

The police told me to find out where James was, to get as much information from him as I could, and to "just act natural." Act natural! I was sick with fear and worry. I could hardly talk coherently because my mind was whirling, and they wanted me to "act natural."

Finally, James did call. "They think you killed Jena!" I said and then pleaded with him to come home.

"I didn't kill her, Mom," he cried out. "I can't give myself up! They will kill me!"

I called the police, and again they said to act natural and find out where he was. To me, acting natural would have been running off into the night, screaming frantically—that was what I wanted to do. However, that was not what they meant; they asked that I act as calmly as possible. They wanted me to get James' exact location and as much information out of him as I could. In reality, "calm" was not how I felt. It was more like shock and terror and anger and sick.

James called back, and he was sure my phone was tapped. It wasn't, but he was not convinced. He said he was leaving and wouldn't be calling again. "Where are you going?" I pleaded, but he wouldn't tell me, which was just as well. I couldn't tell the police something I did not know. A part of me wanted him to come back; the rest of me wanted him to flee to places unknown, as far away as possible. He was freaked out, and so was I.

My pastor and his wife came to my house. They visited with me, comforted me and prayed with me. They wanted me to go home with them, but I could not do that. I had to wait for James to call again, or the police might call, saying they found him.

Finally, everyone left, and I was alone. Nervously, I waited for the phone to ring. Devastated, I sat there praying for James, praying for myself, and praying about the whole mess.

The phone rang at 2 a.m.; it was Don, James' father. "They have James in jail. The police found him in Jackpot," Don whispered, his voice choked with tears. It was a long night fraught with fear, frenzy, no sleep, frustration, anger, and of course, buckets of tears soaking my pillow.

The Anguish of
Being in Jail

5

July 23, 1980: Heartbreak Unspeakable

hey finally let me see James on Tuesday afternoon, three days after he was arrested. He was a very frightened young man. "Mom," he said, "if I had gone to Sunday school and church like you wanted me to, I probably wouldn't be in this mess." What a sad statement but probably a true one. The chances of James' being in this kind of trouble would have been a lot slimmer if he had been involved with church, although this is not always true. Circumstances in our lives can make deep changes in our thought patterns. Even Christians can make huge blunders under duress, and when the pressures and thoughts collide, we can suddenly find a weapon in our hands and a dead body lying at our feet. When we recover from the shock, we wonder how in the world we

16

did that. True, most of us remain in control, but there is a percentage out here in the world that don't keep their thoughts and actions in check.

James chose to hang around a rough crowd of hurting individuals—people who hurt and faced similar issues, just like he did, and who dealt with broken homes and broken hearts.

The first time I visited James in jail, we sat on opposite sides of a glass partition, and we couldn't touch or hug. It was so difficult not to be able to hold and comfort each other. The tears flowed down our faces. Never in all the world did I ever think this would happen to us.

The second visit was better because we were allowed to be in a private room. I sat on James' lap since he felt he was too old to sit on mine. He sat and cried just as he had as a little boy, and I cried right along with him. These were tears of a frightened child and a brokenhearted mother. These tears were the beginning of many more to come, with heartbreak unspeakable.

My pastor preached another sermon titled "A Mother's Right to Cry" because of what I was going through. Yes, a mother has a right to cry. The Lord comes in with His soothing balm, and He applies it to the broken heart. He mops up the tears and comforts us with His voice, His touch, and His song: "He calls us into the garden, and there, where the dew is on the roses, he walks with us and talks with us and calls us His own." This sentence is an excerpt from *the song titled In The Garden*.

I remembered a sermon that my pastor had preached, "God's Grace Is Sufficient," and now I knew that God truly had intended that sermon for me. The Lord sent many people to minister to me during that time. There were so many wonderful phone calls, words of encouragement, letters, and cards. There were calls from people I had forgotten about. The Lord protected me, but James' father received threatening phone calls and scornful passers-by. There were two occasions, however, when I was not treated nicely. Once was when I tried to collect money that was owed to me from someone who had purchased my mobile home. He said, "I didn't know if I wanted to pay you, because of what your son did, but my wife convinced me that it was you I owed the money to, not your son." I was shocked and hurt, but I just had to set it aside. That took some time. The other time was when an acquaintance made a comment to me about James' situation that was unkind. Those times were hurtful, but there were so many more people who treated me kindly that I didn't succumb to the hurtful comments. Words are like arrows that pierce the heart and bleed for a long time.

"You are my Rock and my Fortress. Of whom shall I be afraid? (Psalm 71:3, THE NKJV

A friend from my church came to visit me and brought me some banana bread. She stayed quite a while and was very loving and sympathetic. Later, I learned what a sacrifice it was for her. Her sister had been murdered several years before. I can only imagine the memories this whole situation brought back to her. It was obvious that Jesus had ministered to her and healed her, or she could not have ministered to me so graciously. "I know the Thought that I think toward you, says the Lord, thoughts of peace not of evil to give you a future and a hope." Jeremiah29:11&12 NKJV. Her ministry to me brought great comfort while I was hurting so badly.

It has been said that when you are in crisis, if you have only one supportive person, you can make it through the journey. We all need at least one person to be there for us in the middle of a tragedy. It also has been said that it takes ninety-five affirmations to overcome one hurtful statement. As you can see, there were many comforting words and lots of support to counter the few hurtful words I did encounter.

Some wonderful people walked with me through this journey.

It was during this time that the Lord put two very special people in my life to minister to me and to walk through this time of pain and sorrow. Wayne and Sharon were there all of the time. Sharon called every day and came to the house frequently.

After several days, I returned to work. Because I didn't have a car, I had to walk to work, which was at least a mile and a half. If Wayne and Sharon were going to be out of town, they let me use one of their cars. Sometimes they were able to give me a ride to work.

Wayne had a cleaning business, and Sharon stayed home but also took care of the office for Wayne's business and helped him when he needed an extra hand. They were a team both in the business and in the home. They were active in our church and in the community. The Lord knew who I would need during this time.

My pastor, John Butters, and his wife, Lisa were also support for me. They were always there when I needed them. Often on Sunday after church, they would take me home to have dinner with them. John was more than just a pastor doing what pastors do when someone in the flock needs care. He and Lisa became dear friends to me. Whenever I needed my pastor, he always showed up. I didn't have to call him; he just knew when I needed him. It's the Holy Spirit speaking in that small, still voice, nudging us to do what is needed to be done. He is a great communicator if we will communicate with Him, and listening is half of communicating.

John and Lisa took very good care of me, helping me and protecting me with their love and prayers.

James' father was heartbroken, but he had family support and a few friends but not nearly the support I had. He kept Trace, our youngest son, with him, but our daughter, Maryann, had her own home in Spring Creek, so after a few days at her father's house she went to her home. She was also pregnant with her first child and our first grandchild. This was to become our "joy baby." She was an unwed mother-to-be, but the timing was right. The baby, Todd, was born that November, just before the trial in December. God knew what we would need and turned this untimely pregnancy into a timely birth.

James' grandparents in Karie and in Frenchman Ford were devastated, humiliated, and dismayed. Their precious grandson was suddenly wanted by the law. They had a very hard time with this. Grandparents often think their grandchildren are nearly perfect—they extol the wonderful, smart, beautiful children their grandchildren are. James' transgressions certainly muddied this image. They aged considerably during this period of time.

When it was time for the trial, James' grandmother, Susanna, in Carlin, had to be involved in the testimonies at the trial. She had to testify about what she might have known, but she knew nothing of the situation. Susanna had helped raise James, and it was very difficult for her to be there. She was a strong lady, however, and she did very well during her testimony.

My parents, James' grandparents in Duns Glenn, were not required to be there because they were far removed from the situation. They did come to be with me during the trial, though, and I appreciated them so much for doing this.

The Preliminary Hearing

"Let's Get a Keg and Take It to the Park"

fter James was arrested that early Sunday morning, I began the search for an attorney. The first one I called was a civil attorney who didn't do criminal cases. He referred me to the public defender, whom I never did reach, although I tried several times. I also was referred to a criminal case attorney. James' father and I went to see him, and he kept insisting that we could not afford him. He wanted thousands of dollars, and he said, "I believe James is guilty," which did not build a lot of confidence between client and attorney. Now what did we do? A week went by, and we still did not have an attorney for James—and he needed one now. The next time I was visiting my son, an attorney named Gary came in to talk to James.

He told me, "You have to get a lawyer right away." I told him about calling the public defender and that I was unable to reach him. I also told him about the rude and expensive attorney and said that I did not know anyone else. He said, "I am not trying to influence your choice of lawyers, but I will represent James." When I asked him how much he charged, I was relieved that it was a price range we could manage. I called James' father when I got home, and Don agreed we should hire Gary.

I asked Gary why he was so less expensive than the lawyer who'd told me he thought James was guilty. He said the other attorney hired a lot of people to do his leg work. Gary didn't do that, so he didn't have to charge as much.

The first meeting I had with Gary entailed my telling him all I knew. That sure didn't take long. I didn't know very much about James' friends or where they worked, played, or hung out. I knew very little about James' activities outside of the home.

I learned that I should have refused to speak with the police about details until I had representation from an attorney. I didn't know I could do that, and the police certainly didn't mention it to us. It wasn't illegal that they did not tell us, because they had read James his rights and told him he had the right to an attorney.

A few weeks after retaining Gary, we had the preliminary hearing and everyone there was subpoenaed to testify. This was where I met the district attorney, a young lawyer dressed like Black Bart. His attire was black suits and overcoats or capes. He stood approximately six feet tall and had black hair and brown eyes—a very formidable-appearing young fellow, but he was soft-spoken.

Our attorney, Gary stood about five foot ten and had blond hair and piercing blue eyes. He usually wore brown tweeds and had a confident persona. He spoke firmly and precisely.

While sitting in the outer room, waiting for our turn to testify, a friend of James' spoke up. "It is too bad we can't get a keg of beer and take it to the park to do this."

I thought, *My God, child! That is where all of this began!*

"Be sober, be vigilant, because your adversary, the devil, walks about like a roaring lion, seeking whom he may devour" (1 Peter 5:8. NKJV).

Once all the witnesses were questioned, we were allowed into the courtroom.

At the conclusion of the preliminary hearing, it was determined that James would be bound over for trial. Our hopes of his release were dashed, and I cried.

Terror, Tears, and Hysterics

A few weeks after the preliminary hearing, I picked up the newspaper at work. On the front page, printed in huge capital letters, were words that devastated and terrified me: DA SEEKS DEATH PENALTY FOR JONES.

I raced to the phone and when I finally reached James' attorney, I began to cry and babble into the phone, totally hysterical. Terror had struck, and I wasn't coherent. Gary was finally able to calm me down enough to assure me the DA was not actually seeking the death penalty but just using it as a ploy to keep James incarcerated and dispel any hope of posting bail. All I could think was, *How cruel to do that to us.* I was furious that Gary didn't warn us. Attorney's however, do what they want without thought for the family.

James had been arrested in July, and the trial was set for December. What was I doing during this time? I searched for money for the bail I could not possibly pay. I prayed, cried, went to church, taught Sunday school, and went to work. Life went on as usual—on the outside. Internally, I operated in a state of shock.

I finally broke down one evening at church. People were so surprised, because my outward appearance led them to believe I was always in control. One lady said I was the only person she knew who could "fall into an outhouse and come out smelling like a rose." I also was called "Superwoman," but God was the super in me.

On the inside I was dying. I was isolating the pain and despair inside me, as though putting it into a glass box, which could only be seen but not released. It would not be until later that I could open that glass box of emotions and let it all out. Very few people understood what was going on inside my heart, and truthfully, I didn't understand it myself. Every time the newspaper headlines announced another decision made from the DA's office, my heart wrenched, and I shriveled up into a fetal position on the inside, which was only evident to God.

The Lord God carried me through this time, and I clung to his promises and to His words, "His grace is sufficient." I operated on autopilot to get through the day.

Actually, it was my heavenly Father carrying me through, and He is very much alive.

The trial started on December 8 and lasted for two weeks. I was called to the stand. The DA asked question after question, rephrasing them to see if he could get me to say what he wanted me to say. I finally said, "I don't know what you want me to say." The judge interceded and said, "She has answered the questions, so now move on." I wish I could remember the questions he repeatedly asked me, but I can't.

While I was sitting in the waiting room before my turn to get on the stand, a lady approached me and asked me how I was managing so well. I showed her my book of God's promises and said it helped to keep me sane during all of this. She nodded her head in agreement and said, "No wonder." God's word brings comfort and hope.

Another time after I had testified, a man asked me about my education. I told him and asked why he wanted to know. He said he knew that one of the mothers was a schoolteacher and wondered if it was me. I told him I had some formal education, but I was leaning on the love of Jesus Christ to keep me going.

Surprisingly, a sheriff's deputy perjured himself and lied about certain evidence in question. At the lunch break, my friend Wayne went to there, looked around, and came back to tell me there was all sorts of debris that could have been used as a weapon, which James said was there. This was in reference to part of my son's testimony, where he had stated he had gotten into a fight with a Mexican and said he had hit him with a board and knocked him down. This area was at the Flag pole on a hill overlooking Dun's Glenn.

I told Wayne to contact the DA and tell him what he had found. When court reconvened, the DA called another deputy to testify about the area in question. They never did anything to the deputy who lied. He lied about going to the flag pole area and stating there was nothing up there that could be used as a weapon.

When we were at the pretrial arraignment, they asked me lots of questions, which I answered as truthfully as I knew how. Before the main trial, I received a transcript of everything they'd asked me, along with my answers.

After the trial was over, I picked up that transcript and read it for the first time. I had answered the questions at the trial almost verbatim to the way I'd answered at the preliminary hearing. When you tell the truth, you don't have to worry about remembering what you said.

Finally, when trial was over, the jury then was left to deliberate and determine the guilt or innocence of my son. That's when the tortuous waiting began for me. They deliberated for seven hours, as I waited, not knowing if my son would be set free or be incarcerated for the rest of his life.

The jury returned, and the head juror stood and read a small piece of paper, saying, "We the jury find the defendant, James Jones, guilty of murder in the first degree." The sentence was life in prison without parole.

I have tried to remember the details of verdict and sentencing but I can't. Someday I may recall them, but for now I can remember only that my entire body went numb. The tears began to flow, and my brain turned to jelly. Breathing became a conscious effort. It took great effort to walk down the enclosed stairs down from the courtroom to the jail because I was trying not to faint. The sheriff held one of my arms, and my pastor held the other. My pastor talked to me the whole time, but I didn't understand a word he said. To this day, I don't have any idea what he said to me—it was all a blur.

I do remember looking over the balcony before we went down the stairs and seeing the district attorney walk away. He had no victory in his gait. He had won the battle, but the war within weighed heavily on him. I learned later that he was a Christian, and he told me it was one of the hardest things he had ever done. He said he was worried about me and hoped I was going to be okay. His concern for me was very touching. All through the trial, I couldn't be angry with him. He was just doing his job, and I would have wanted him to work just as hard for me if it had been my daughter who was killed. Not everyone felt that way, but he wasn't the cause of this mess; he was only trying to bring justice for the other family.

Run, Baby, Run!

James Escapes Jail

n January 29, 1981, the month after James' trial, he had to return to court for sentencing. After the formality of sentencing was done, he was escorted back to the jail to await the day of transport to the California State Prison

The actual day or the hour when transport will occur is not revealed to avoid attempted escapes or someone trying to kill the convict.

The night of the formal sentencing, however, James escaped from the jail. Throughout his incarceration, one jailer felt it was his duty to torture James with horrendous details of what awaited him when he got to the prison. This jailer also told me these same horrible details.

As soon as I stepped out of the courthouse, where the jail was housed, the Lord reassured me that He was in control, and He would take care of James. I tried to convey this to James, but at that time, he didn't trust God, and his fears overrode anything I said. I certainly understood why a seventeen-year-old boy would be terrified. Prisons are a horrible place for anyone, but young ones are in danger from the older ones, who abuse, rape, and terrorize them and hold them in bondage.

It is cruel and ugly, and most of the guards do little to prevent this. While young men are in bondage as a sex slave, they abuse them incessantly. When they are through with these boys, they are turned over to others to use or, in a lot of cases, they arrange for their deaths, but no one knows who did it. Having been told all of this, James decided being shot would be a kinder death.

That evening, James asked to make a phone call, and the jailer let him out of his cell. James grabbed an industrial-size mop and beat the jailer over the head with it, seriously wounding him, which put him in the hospital due to the injuries. Surprisingly, James never tried to get any of the guns—the guns were locked in a gun safe, and James didn't have time to find the right keys.

James ran to his ex-stepfather's house and took his car. His stepsisters were there, and they gave him the keys when he asked for them. At no time did his actions or attitude display violence toward them. They explained later that he was scared and had an extreme desire to flee.

He drove to an outlying area where his sister lived and stopped to see her. Then he went on farther toward the mountains, where there was no passable route over the mountains during the winter. In the summer, the roads are clear.

My daughter called me to tell me James had escaped. I was so shocked and in a state of disbelief that I called the jail to confirm what she had told me. Again the tears were flowing.

"Yes, James has escaped," I was told, "and the jailer was injured."

I hung up, shaken to the core. Again, I was fearful—more so than before, as I was sure they would kill him this time. My heart raced, my brain fogged, and I wanted to scream. If I had had my car, I probably would have gone to look for him. I would have been searching in the wrong places, though, because I believed he would take the freeway. I never imagined he would head for a dead end. "Oh, run, baby. run!" my heart cried.

I called Wayne and Sharon, who had stood by me through this ongoing saga. They came over right away. I also called James' attorney who had left a voice message to call his secretary, which I did. She called Gary before she came to my house.

Gary called me and wanted to know if James would hurt his family. I told him he would not. "Why do you think James would do that?" I asked.

"If clients don't get cleared of the charges," Gary said, "often they try to retaliate against their attorney."

After my friends arrived, we tried to think of some way James could have left me a message. I had his suit from his court appearances in the upstairs closet. We raced upstairs and searched the jacket pockets. Sure enough, there was a note to me from James.

"Mom, by the time you find this I will be dead. I would rather be shot and killed than go to prison and be raped, mutilated, and killed!" Again, this mother's tears flowed, as well as my friend's, as the fear and pain took over again.

I had called James' father, Don, when I first found out that James had escaped. He said he would stay home in case James came there. After we had found the note and I calmed down, I called Don to tell him what we found. Don was as upset as I was. "I will call with any information as soon as I get it," I told him, and he agreed to do the same. Here we were again, trying to stay calm in a hurricane of fear and dread. The fear had me by the throat and was squeezing hard. Emotions ran high and clear thinking eluded me. When would life ever return to some kind of normalcy?

James' juvenile probation officer, Mr. Clarence, appeared at my door, with his gun strapped to his hip. He wondered if I had heard from James. He said he had some trouble finding me because I had moved.

I don't think James knew where I was living. He never came to my house. If he had, I would have wanted to tell him to run far away and never come back. I probably would not have done that but that would have been my want to. I told Mr. Clarence I had not seen or heard from James. I did tell him that James' sister had seen him. As Mr. Clarence was leaving, I begged him, "Please don't shoot James!" He said he wouldn't, and somehow I believed him.

The phone rang at 2 a.m., and a police officer assured me that James was safely captured—James had driven the car into a snow bank and had started walking. He was suffering from hypothermia when the police found him. He was getting warm—and he also was back in jail.

This time I cried tears of relief. I called Don—the police had called him, too—and we talked for a while, expressing our fear of what was going to happen to James. We tried to give some comfort to one another over the phone. When I got off the phone, my tears came like a flood.

After a short time, James was back in court, facing new charges of escaping jail and injuring the jailer. This time he had a different judge, and he was not a merciful judge. Out of a possible twenty years, he sentenced James to an additional sixteen years, to run concurrently with the previous sentence of life without parole.

This time the authorities didn't waste any time. After the sentencing, they loaded him into a van and headed for Carson City. They were not taking the chance that he might escape again. It was a tearful, heartrending farewell. We would have no contact with James for several weeks as the prison did an evaluation, which would determine where he would be placed in the prison system. He was incarcerated in the minimum security part of the prison for a number of months until the evaluation was completed.

I Fall to Pieces Like a Broken Toy

When it was safe, the Lord let the glass box shatter, and my emotions were released. I couldn't make decisions; I went to work, but I couldn't focus. I felt disoriented, and I wept. All of a sudden, I was like a broken toy, with my inner pieces strewn about. In desperation one night, I called my ex-husband, who lived across town. I asked him to take me to the hospital. He sleepily agreed, and he dropped me off at the emergency room. When the hospital discharged me, I had to call Craig again to take me home. He wasn't happy with me, but he obliged.

The next day I went to work and proceeded to fall apart there. I still didn't have my car, so I started to walk home. A friend drove by and stopped to see if I needed a ride. When I got home, I called Sharon, and she came over and took me to the doctor. He told me he would have admitted me to the hospital the night before if I had told the emergency room nurse to call him. He wrote orders to admit me to the hospital. Sharon took me to the hospital, and a nurse took me to a private room. I found out later it was the room for people who are mentally ill. I was mentally stressed, and that was close enough. The doctor limited my visitors to just a few people—my pastor, my friend Sharon, my youngest daughter, and her father. My oldest daughter, who was part of the ongoing stress, was not allowed to visit. She was furious, but I discovered this only later.

I couldn't have phone calls. I was in isolation to ensure that I got adequate rest. After a few days, my doctor released me from the hospital, but I went home with him, spending several days with him and his wife, who was my friend. They owned a ranch ten miles from town, and I loved to go out there. We did chores, took care of the animals, drank tea, and visited. It was good, but I wanted to go home. They wanted to keep me longer, but I was ready to leave. Once I got home, reality hit hard. My life was going to be different forever. I fell to pieces again. The pressures were still there, and my coping ability definitely was not. I was armed with a strong medication to help me sleep, which was dangerous in the emotional shape I was in.

Tears, Pills, and Desperation 10

I Want to Escape

came home from work early because I could not cope, and I was in tears. I decided I was going to end it all—I could not live like this. I grabbed my bottle of pills and headed for my bedroom. I lay on the bed, clutching the bottle of pills. I began to tell the Lord all about my life—how I had prayed to Him ever since I was a ten-year-old child. I didn't know about Jesus then, but my granny had a poster with the Lord's Prayer on it. My mom said she prayed that prayer every night when she went to bed, so I did too.

I told Him how I seemed to know He was there. I told Him I always believed in Him. I was hurting badly, and I couldn't go on this way. I told Him of my fears and my despair. Then warmth, like a warm bath, came upon me. It was so soothing, and I began to cry softly-tears of relief and healing. His love was pouring out all over me. I got up from the bed, went into the bathroom, and flushed the pills down the toilet, never to need them again. God says, "I Am the God that heals you!" and yes, He does, and yes, He did.

And He said to me, "My grace is sufficient for you; for my strength is made perfect in weakness" (2 Corinthians 12:9, NKJV). I got up from my bed and began to rejoice in my healing, rejoicing at what my Lord had done for me, and sharing the good news.

I called my friend Sharon and told her everything that had happened. She was excited and so happy for me. She came over and we went out for coffee. The Lord gave me hope and renewed my faith and my joy. Never again have I been in that mind-set, thinking I needed to take my life—a terrible place to be! When we lose hope and faith, there seems to be no reason to live and that is when people take their life. The Lord restored those things in me and has made my faith stronger in Him. My heart aches when I hear of someone taking his life. The mentally ill often take their life because they cannot endure the mental torment that goes on in their heads. The cacophony of voices becomes so loud that they cannot hear the truth. They lose hope and in search of peace, they take their life. Other people get desperate because of things that happen to them or to a loved one. They lose sight of hope and choose death because the pain is too great. Pain, whether physical or emotional, can be so overwhelming that death seems the only escape.

Prison for Life

A ⊤ ⌒f Freedom

he first time I went to see James after he was sent to prison, I was so surprised at how accepting he was of being there. It took me a while to understand that he was experiencing more freedom than he had had for almost a year. He could walk out to the yard, he could smoke when he wanted, and he had a certain degree of freedom. It was a big improvement over the jail. Before I finally grasped that concept, I was a little irritated at his acceptance. I honestly don't know what I expected him to do. I certainly had to adjust my attitude. I had no idea what to expect on that first visit or the extent of the emotions that would race through my mind and body.

Visiting a loved one in prison is a shock to one's sensibilities. Once you step into the prison environment, you are subject to physical searches. How personal it gets is determined by how much of a problem they perceive you might be. It is still uncomfortable for me, after 20 years. I'm required to remove my shoes, get patted down, and loosen my bra so they can shake it enough to make sure I am not carrying anything in it. Some people have to endure internal searches but thankfully, I have not. Personal space is definitely invaded and a sense of fear permeates you.

Of course, a female officer searches women, and a male officer searches men, but that doesn't mean it is any more comfortable. They still touch you, and they definitely are not your friend. It's impersonal on their part but very personal for you. Just think of someone you do not know, walking up to you and patting you down from the shoulders down past your bottom and then shaking your bra or the waist of your pants and underwear. It's done from outside your clothes, but there's a natural instinct to rebel against that, even though you know you can't.

Keys, belts, and jewelry or watches are left in a tray at the gatehouse. Wedding rings are okay. Women are not allowed to wear jeans, shorts, or halter tops; long skirts or dresses are okay. You are allowed to bring money for drinks and snacks from the vending machines, but this must be in rolls of wrapped quarters, which are opened and put into a plastic tray. You have to ask the guard to open the restroom for you every time. The whole time you are visiting, you are watched. Some guards are friendly and courteous, and some are cold and barely tolerate you. There are no "warm fuzzies" in prison visits.

Walking across the yard from the gatehouse gives a very uneasy feeling. The whole area around the prison is fenced in razor wire. This is to discourage inmates from going over the top. Guard towers are placed strategically around the area. The guards have guns, and they know how to use them. There are no trees, lawns, flowers, or shrubs; there is only hard white concrete and desolation.

On one of my visits, I asked if I could wear my sunglasses until we got to the visitors building, because the blazing sun reflecting against the barren white concrete was very hurtful to my eyes. The first day, the lady guard was congenial and said, "Yes. You can just leave them at the desk upon entering the visiting room." The next day I had a different lady guard; she was very rude and even angry that I would ask and inconvenience her. "I don't have time to watch over your glasses," she snapped at me. "I can't be responsible for your stuff!" What an unexpected response! The male guard who was behind the desk just looked at me and raised his eyebrows. He had been there the day before, and he was surprised at this guard's response, but he never said anything. When I told James about it, he said the inmates did not respect that guard, but the other female guard, who also had a higher status, was highly respected. She was tough but fair and always treated the inmates with a modicum of respect if they were respectful. I liked her, and she even displayed some humor. What a difference in personality and attitude. Not all of the guards are rude, mean-spirited, or vindictive, but a number of them would be much happier working somewhere else—and so would the inmates. Some guards are as corrupt as the people they are guarding, and they incite problems.

Entering the prison domain is entering a different world. The visits with loved one are always cautious and tense. You are allowed to hug when you first come in and when you leave. You can hold hands on top of the table as long as your hands are in plain view. When you leave and drive out of the gate, the tension begins to leave, and you realize that your whole being has been tense. Often, tears flow as people leave, and James has said that after the visits, everyone feels down. The visits are good, but the feelings of loss come crowding in as soon as the loved ones are gone. It is painful both for those who are left behind and those who are leaving. There is no balm to apply to these wounds, except the Lord Jesus. He knows and experienced those wound on the cross for us. He is our only comfort and peace during these times. We need to depend on Him to see us through. Jesus said, "When you visit the prisoner or give someone a cup of cold water, you have ministered to me."

Ely, California. is truly the coldest, most unyielding, desolate place in the whole system, as I experienced it.

James said this was true.

Prison Life/ Playing in the Devil's Playground

Evil Is the Name of the Game

hen James was finally transferred to another prison, he was placed in a prison that was set up as protective custody for prisoners who needed protection for various reasons; being a youth was one of those reasons. There was a certain amount of protection, but very dangerous. He seemed to be okay there. If he wasn't, he didn't tell me. Prison is the devil's playground, and evil is the name of the game. Some were there to be protected from gang members. There are riots, fights, knifings, beatings, and general disorder, which gets the guards attention, and if the mayhem doesn't stop, then buckshot flies, followed by real bullets if the buckshot doesn't work.

James and his friend were in the midst of this mayhem when the buckshot started flying, and James got some in his leg and knee. His knee was permanently damaged. Even if someone is not participating, if he is in the area when trouble breaks out, he likely will get hurt or even killed.

Just recently, James shared some of the horror he has gone through while he has been in prison. He has always tried to protect me from the worst of the brutality in prison. He told me he has had to fight for his life on many occasions.

He ended up in the hospital on several occasions after being beaten severely by other inmates.

All I can say is that he has survived all of that, and his life is relatively quiet now—I think. I trust God to keep him in His care, just as I trusted Him before. In many ways, He has kept James when it looked impossible. When James told me these things, I thought about the apostle Paul in the Bible and how he suffered much torture and was left for dead several times. His was not an easy life, but he believed his Lord and Savior was with him in all his trials.

The following happened after James had been at a medium-security prison in California. After a number of years, he was transferred to Ely, California, where the "lifers" were sent. Life without parole got you a free ride to this prison. It is a very lonely, desolate place. There is a feeling of hopelessness there, and some people are very dangerous. The prison is out in the desert, with nothing around but alkali, a white earth substance that allows very little to grow, and a few scrubby sage brush. If a prisoner was to escape, there is nowhere to hide, and he would either freeze or die of heat stroke—or get shot. Not a kind place to be.

James was there for ten years and then, by the grace of God and a physical ailment, he was moved back to Lovelock. He was having some heart issues and surprisingly, they moved him. A lot of times prisoners may have a cardiac arrest, and they die. No one tends to them in time. You don't hear about that on the news.

The other important thing for James was that he had parents who were involved with him. We visited him and wrote letters, and he called us. We had enough family involvement that no one would let his serious health issues slide. That would bring a lawsuit, and the prison systems don't like the outside world to know what is going on.

When James was moved back to Lovelock, he had more freedom and projects to occupy his time. These projects started as hobby/craft classes, but the inmates were given credit for completing them, and this was added to their "good time" file, which helps reduce their time in prison when they come up for parole. James was able to complete a number of these classes. After a while, he was asked to facilitate some of these classes. Each class earned him certificates as they were completed. He also designed and implemented a new program—making guitars. He was very excited about doing this. He was able to find a store that agreed to sell these guitars. Unfortunately, the chains of command at the prison changed, and these classes were closed.

Throughout most of the time James has been incarcerated, he has been able to learn the business of "law clerk" or jailhouse lawyer. Out here, the profession is called paralegal. He is very good at it and loves it. He actually understands all that legal jargon that confounds most of us.

Issues of the Heart

When I Called upon God, He Was There

While in Ely, James developed heart problems and a lung problem. He had trouble breathing. It was sporadic but scary, and it became more persistent. The prison would not do the MRI to diagnose the problem. Unfortunately, I did not have the finances to pay for an MRI. I had been praying for provisions for this, but nothing seemed to happen.

One day, my friend Debi and her mother, Beverly, came over to my home. Debi asked how James was doing, and I explained the situation about James' health. I asked for continued prayer for a solution. She already knew we were held up from doing anything due to the inadequate finances. I wasn't going to mention it, but she brought it up. She and I had been close friends for some time, but I hardly knew her mother. A few hours after they left, Debi called me and said her mother felt that the Lord wanted her to provide the money for the MRI. I was shocked—and overjoyed! The tears of joy start falling every time I tell this story. Beverly heard the need, and she heard the Lord urging her to provide the money for the procedure.

I sent the money to James, and the procedure was completed. The MRI revealed the problem—James had inhaled a small bug or a seed into his lung. The lung tissue had grown around it, encapsulating it. This was causing his lung to spasm. James said, "Mom, immediately after they removed it, I could breathe. I hadn't been able to breathe like that for quite a while!" Again, the Lord was looking after James. God used this wonderful woman to provide what James needed.

It also was at this time that James turned his life over to the Lord and became a born-again Christian. I could not believe that he would do that—he'd said he never would—but he was very emphatic about it. He would not go to the Bible studies, even though they were available. He said the other inmates used the Bible studies and committing their lives to the Lord to make it look good on their records. James watched them, and he couldn't see any changes in their lives. They still acted and spoke just as badly, just as ornery and unkind as before. He judged them as liars.

When we say the Lord has entered our heart and He has changed us, the world around us should be able to see change rather quickly—not perfection but definitely some change. Some people have a lot farther to come than others do, so we need to be careful in our assessment. When you live around them all of the time, you would know if there was a change.

Again, the Lord was there and in His timing, James' life changed. I asked him why he had changed his mind, and he answered, "I thought I was going to die." It really has changed his life, and he doesn't talk rough like he once did, nor does he rage and rant like he once did. It is for real, and he relies on the Lord to help him.

God says in His word, "Train up a child in the way he should go, and when he is old he will not depart from it." James knew where to go when he needed what God had to offer. He was raised in the church, and although he rebelled against it like the prodigal son, he knew where to go when he needed help.

James' sentence was commuted from life without parole to life with parole. Praise the Lord! The Lord does some of His best work in the devil's backyard. Oh, how the devil hates that when God trumps over him and takes what that evil one meant for harm and turns it around for good.

Seven years later, James is still in prison, but I believe he will be released in God's timing. I believe the Lord is going to do that, just as He has taken care of James every step of the way.

Jeremiah 29:11 says, "For I know the thoughts that I think toward you, says the Lord, thoughts of peace and not of evil, to give you a future and a hope."

Through this journey, the Lord has used it and me to minister to others. Through it all, God was and is always there. He is still watching over James.

Grief and Dying in Fiery Circumstances

14

Trials in the Midst of Fire

While this journey of James' was taking place, another tragedy also was taking place. James' oldest stepsister, Nina, and her husband, Brad, along with her sister, Janet, and her husband, Jimmy, and their mechanic traveled to Arizona to race their car. This was September 1, 1980, Labor Day weekend, after James was arrested in July. This also was the day we were going to celebrate our youngest daughter's birthday at my house. Her dad, Craig, was coming also. Although we were divorced, we remained civil to each other to help keep things as normal as we could for May. Craig, however, called to tell me they wouldn't be over for cake and ice cream.

"Why?" I exclaimed.

"Because Nina and Brad were killed in a car accident, and I am still waiting to hear what has happened to Janet and Jonah."

My heart sank, and I could hardly talk. I had raised Nina and Janet for a number of years. "Oh, Craig I am so sorry!"

"I have to get off the phone so they can call me about Janet and Jonah. I'll call back."

I couldn't believe tragedy had struck so soon and in the same family. I was having a hard time wrapping my mind around the conversation I had just experienced. It had been just a month since we had just gone through James being arrested—and now this!

On the kids' return trip from Arizona, their bus began having engine problems, so they pulled off to the side of the road. They used the bus to pull the trailer for the car and to haul the fuel and extra parts. Janet and Jonah and the mechanic were in the bus. Brad and Nina had their car and had gone into town to get what they needed for the bus. They couldn't get parts that day and had to return the next day. They returned to where the bus was parked and parked in front of it. Instead of going back to town and getting a motel for everyone, they decided to sleep in their vehicles, which turned into a disaster. During the night, a driver of an eighteen-wheeler fell asleep at the wheel, drifted across the road, and ran on top of Brad and Nina's car and into the bus, setting everything on fire. It killed Brad and Nina immediately.

The phone rang, and it was Craig. "Jonah got out. There's no information on how badly Janet has been hurt, but she is alive. The car, bus, and racecar were consumed by the fire because of the high octane fuel they had in the bus for the racecar. No news on the mechanic at this time." He hung up, and I call Sharon and Wayne. They had just heard the news from the church. They came over, and we prayed for all of us.

The phone rang again, and Craig said, "Janet has a broken collar bone and some burns, but she will be okay. A friend in our church has a plane, and May and I are flying down to Texas."

"Do you want me to go with you?" I asked.

"That is up to you."

"No, you tell me if you want me to go with you."

"I guess you could," Craig said.

"I'll get ready. You can pick me up. Maryann wants to go, too." Maryann was my pregnant daughter.

Our friend had a small plane, so we were going to fly to an airport that accommodated small planes, and family members would pick us up there when we arrived in Texas. The flight was uneventful, except Craig and my older daughter got sick. May and I didn't get airsick, but we felt a different kind of sick because of the tragedy.

When we arrived, family members whisked us off to the major airport where Janet, Jonah, and the mechanic were disembarking from the plane. Jo had her right arm in a sling and several superficial burns on her face and arm. Jonah had managed to get everyone out of the bus with just a few superficial burns on his hands. They fell into our arms, and we all sobbed and hung on to each other.

Janet and Nina's mother, Shanna, and Craig were devastated but relieved that Janet was going to be okay. Jonah's mom and dad had gone to Arizona to identify the bodies. The kids were so badly burned, they decided to have the remains cremated there. Talk about a mother's and father's right to cry! Shanna's husband and I were as devastated as their parents. When Craig and I married, all four girls were home with him. Now, the two oldest, Nina and Janet, were married to brothers, and they lived in Texas. Darby and Juanita, the two younger ones, were single, and they also lived in Texas. Our youngest, May, lived in Dun's Glenn and spent time with both Craig and me since we had divorced.

This was a sad, horrific, mind-boggling day, and there was no way to make it a happy day for May, except to celebrate the return of her sister and brother-in-law— definitely reason to celebrate but not with birthday cake.

The days leading up to the memorial service were tear-filled, difficult days. Every time family members arrived from out of state or out of town, the tears flowed all over again. On the day of the memorial service, everyone had arrived at the funeral home except Janet and Jonah, Juanita and Darby, and Shanna, the girls' mother. We thought they would be there soon and the service could begin, but this was not to be. We waited and waited and then waited some more. Where were they? There were no cell phones yet, so we couldn't just call. Someone called from the pastor's office, but no one was answering the phone. Finally, the minister wanted to know if we should start without them. Craig said, "Absolutely not."

Finally, they arrived, and the service began. After the service we found out the reason for the delay. The dress Janet had chosen to wear would not work—she couldn't get it over her head because of her broken collar bone. They finally found a blouse and skirt they could make work. They were already distressed, and Janet's struggling to get dressed just made it worse. They were very upset about it all.

In all of this, we had to inject some humor, at the expense of my oldest daughter, Maryann. She was six months pregnant and very large. We were sleeping at Nina and Brad's house, and May, Maryann and I were sharing a king-size water bed. May, being the smallest, slept in the middle. May and I would get into bed, and it would slosh a bit. Then Maryann would get in and nearly wash me out of bed! Because she was so heavy, she pushed all the water in the mattress, along with May and me, to the other side of the bed. Every night, I had to hang on to the edge of the bed to keep from being washed out of bed. We would laugh and laugh! "Laughter does a heart good, like a medicine." Isn't that the truth? Everyone and everything was so serious and sad, it was good to have a moment of laughter.

Maryann's Story   *15*

Schizophrenia: Her Battle with a Broken Brain

Maryann is a sweet lady who has had to deal with hard things in her life. When she was five years old, her father and I divorced. This turned her world upside down. This change affected Maryann and her two brothers for the rest of their lives.

After a short time, I remarried, and this took them deeper into a troubled life. Their older stepsisters were jealous and envious of them, because my children's father was very generous with our children. Because of this, their stepsisters did their best to make life hard for them. Their father and I tried to keep gifts fair, but actually gifts were not the real issue. The issue was that my stepdaughters wanted their mother and father to be reunited. In spite of the fact that both parents were remarried, the girls wanted that desperately and did all they could to cause chaos in the marriages. They hoped against hope that my children and I and their mother's spouse would leave, and their parents could again be married. Divorce is so hard on children.

As time went on, their individual troubles escalated, and it began to affect Maryann in an even more sinister way. I am not saying the stress caused her mental health to deteriorate, but it helped bring it to pass. As she grew older, she became more troubled. I thought it was her reaction to being a teenager, and she was just following in the footsteps of her troubled older sisters, as they grew more rebellious and became involved with drugs. This all happened as her brother James was wandering around in his troubled world. The years from 1975 until 1989 were years of drama and trauma in the lives of these children and in our lives as their parents.

The drug scene was in high gear, and there seemed to be more young people using marijuana and other mind-altering drugs. Hard rock music was their music, and it contributed to the young people's struggles. I remember one song in particular had a phrase in it about being "on the highway to hell"—more truth than poetry to that phrase for this young generation. Drugs, hard rock music, and rebellion were part of the "Age of Aquarius". The '70s were different from any decade we had previously experienced. They were the years of anti-establishment, combat boots, long hair for both men and women, and living in communes. "Peace" was the logo for life. It was a very different lifestyle and one that parents would never have imagined possible. This was also the era of the Vietnam War, a war that affects people to this day, leaving many with broken brains, broken bodies, broken dreams, and suffering the results of Agent Orange—germ warfare.

As Maryann got older, she would disappear for days at a time. At sixteen years old, she would catch rides with truck drivers to travel to various states. Sometimes she got rides back home, and sometimes she called for money to get home. It is amazing she survived those trips. After one of her many trips, she walked into my workplace and informed me she was pregnant. I wasn't exactly surprised, as I believed it was bound to happen.

I was single at that time, so I told her to contact Social Services, as I had no means of helping her. She did, and that was the beginning of her journey through the Social Services system, and she learned how to use it very well. I should have learned something about using the system as well, but I didn't. In later years, I wished I had.

I had no idea that my daughter was mentally ill. I thought she was being rebellious and ornery. She was eighteen and pregnant, and as time went on, she became harder to get along with. Any word or action could set her off on a tirade of yelling and cussing, and I was the target. I thought her hormones were messed up due to the pregnancy, and I told her she should never get pregnant again, as it affected her whole being. I also told her, "You had better take good care of this baby, because you aren't taking very good care of yourself. I will take the baby away from you if you don't take proper care of him."

Her first child, my first grandchild, was born four months after James was incarcerated for allegedly murdering a fourteen-year-old girl. This new baby was our "joy baby" who brought joy into our lives when everything looked so bleak.

Maryann had already faced numerous trials herself and was incarcerated in the reform school for girls when she was fifteen. She was already mentally ill, but we didn't know that. She really needed medical help, not jail. Then James was in major trouble and in jail, and now she was a mother when she was just a child. Just because children are eighteen does not mean they are adults. I tried to help Maryann with the baby, and she did love her baby, but she was not capable of caring for him. Throughout the first six years of her baby's life, I rescued him many times. If she wanted to go somewhere and didn't want to take him, she would leave him alone. I would become very angry with her and lecture her about the danger of leaving him alone—I still didn't know she was ill.

Six years after she gave birth to her first baby, Maryann became pregnant again. This time she was worse than before—I actually could see her getting worse, even before she became pregnant.

It was during this pregnancy that Bill, my husband, and I moved from Idaho to Oregon state. We invited Maryann to come with us, because I was concerned about her, my grandson, and the new baby that was coming soon. When it was near her due date, I went to be with Maryann, but that was a difficult time for both of us. There was no getting along with her, so I stayed with friends until the night she went into labor. Soon, she had a baby boy, weighing almost nine pounds, with lots of dark hair and lusty lungs. I stayed for a few days after Maryann and the baby came home, and then I went back home. Two months later, I got a phone call from Maryann. She was in the hospital and asked if I would come to get the boys.

When Maryann went to the doctor for her two-month checkup, he gave her an antidepressant to help her with what he thought was postpartum blues. She went home and took all the pills at one time. Todd, her six-year-old, had to call 911. The social worker was with Maryann at the hospital, and she thought Maryann could care for the children at home for a couple of days until we could go down on the weekend to get the children.

This was the first step in finding out just what my daughter had been dealing with most of her life—from the time she was ten, which we discovered by looking at her childhood pictures.

When we got there, we stayed overnight with Maryann and the children. When we first arrived, they were sitting outside on the lawn, talking with a neighbor. As I gazed at my oldest grandson, Todd, he looked like a shriveled up old man. I guess I was looking at the inner Todd, because he obviously looked like a six-year-old on the outside. It was God giving me a glimpse of how this little boy felt on the inside. He had been through so much and had so much responsibility thrust on him, with the new baby and his mother. He told me, "I usually can handle her." No six-year-old should have to "handle" his mother.

During the night, Maryann was up and down all night. It made for a very restless night for us all. After breakfast, we packed up and got ready to leave. She informed us that we were not taking her children. Being the impatient person that I am and her mother, I told her that indeed I was taking the children. That, of course, just inflamed the already volatile situation even more. Thank God, my patient husband took over the situation and finally convinced Maryann to let us take them and also to write a letter of permission so we could seek medical help for the children if we needed it. We promised to bring the children back as soon as she was feeling better and was able to care for the children.

After we left with the two children, Maryann really fell apart and was admitted into a hospital in Boise, where they had care for the mentally ill. We didn't have any phone contact with her that entire month. We continued to care for our grandchildren and let Todd be the little boy that he was. For most of that month, when we weren't out doing something, he just sat and watched a children's station on the TV that had gentle cartoons. He finally met a little Japanese boy about his age, and they began to play together on a regular basis.

One day the phone rang; it was Maryann's doctor. He was almost rude and not especially kind with the news he was delivering. He informed me, "You need to adopt those children out, because she can't take care of them." He didn't tell me what her health problem was. I insisted he tell me why she couldn't take care of her children and why I needed to place them up for adoption. He gave me the "matter of privacy" mumbo-jumbo. I told him, "You are telling me I need to place my grandchildren up for adoption, and you won't tell me what is wrong with my daughter? I want to know right now what her diagnosis is." He finally told me she was schizophrenic, and she could not care for the children, and then he hung up! He never once mentioned where we might get her some help with everyday living. Furious and shocked hardly covers the way I felt. I thought Maryann just had postpartum blues and perhaps would need medicine for depression. This meant another change in the meaning of "normal," whatever normal was.

When Bill, my husband, got home from work, we talked about the doctor's comments, and we agreed we would not allow anyone to adopt the children. We were young enough that we would be able to raise them. Bill has been a wonderful grandpa/dad to these boys. They think he walks on water—I do too.

My daughter went to California to live with her father and stepmother. They thought they could deal with her better than they could with the children. That did not prove to be true. The longer she lived with them, the harder it became. Her stepmother did not understand mental illness at all (we didn't either), and her attempt to handle it made life hard for everyone there. Maryann missed me and her children and was not functioning well with her stepmom. This caused her to attempt suicide several times. She was placed in the mental hospital in California, where she lived until I went to there and brought her home with me. I began to look into mental health care in Oregon, where we lived. Fortunately, I found a mental health facility just a few blocks from where we lived. After visiting with her father, we agreed to move her to Oregon, where we were living.

We got her into the mental health care, but she didn't want to go to the group home. Unfortunately, that turned out to be a big mistake. It would have saved all of us a lot of heartache, tears, and stress if we would have insisted she go into a group home at that time.

When we moved the children up to live with us, we didn't have any insurance for us or the children. Had I learned how to use Social Services, I would have had some place to go to get help with the kids. I later learned that I was qualified to get all kinds of help, including money and Medicaid and food stamps, if I needed them, because I was raising someone else's children. What a big help that would have been. Much later, I was able to get Aid to Dependent Children and Medicaid for them. I never needed food stamps.

When Maryann moved in with us and persuaded us to let her live with us, she went to Social Services and got all of those things right away. It was a relief to have the kids covered. It also meant scholarships for the kids when it came time to sign them up for sports and other events they wanted to do that we wouldn't have been able to provide.

Now Maryann was living with us, and even though she was able to get some things done, she was so heavily medicated she couldn't do much. After a while, the doctors at the mental health care facility began to lower her dosage so she could be more motivated. She went there every day and participated in activities, ate lunch, and went out and about with her social worker. This was nice for her and much better than just sitting around all day doing nothing. She could go to the library, which was just around the corner from where we lived, and take the bus to go to Cross Roads, a shopping area a few blocks from where we lived.

She lived with us for two years. The first year was okay, but after that, things began to deteriorate. She took herself off all of her medications and became very volatile and aggressive toward me. We had some serious altercations that eventually involved the police; she had to be her removed from our home. She went from our house to an apartment that the mental health facility helped her find. That was another trail of tears. She would forget to take her medicine and then she would take too much. One time she was so miserable and helpless that she called people and invited them to her funeral. One person called me and I went to see her. When I saw how sick she was, I told her, "Mommy knows best. You need to go to the hospital where you can get some help." I took her to the local hospital, but unfortunately, we had to wait for hours before we were able to see someone.

If you have a broken bone or are bleeding, you get help right away. If you have a broken brain, you wait for hours with no one acknowledging you. I was afraid she would leave before she got help. Finally, she was admitted to the hospital, where she stayed for a month, but then she left. They couldn't hold her against her will. However, we did get another diagnosis: she was not only schizophrenic; she also was bipolar, which accounted for behavior not associated with schizophrenia—inappropriate reactions to situations, such as laughing when nothing was funny. Now she had another disorder, as well as having to deal with not having her children, hearing voices, and trying to deal with what was real and what was not. In one of her most lucid moments, she said, "Mom, it is terrible when you can't trust your brain." What a sad statement and so true for her and the many others who deal with mental illness on a daily basis. No wonder they often choose not to fight the battle anymore and take their lives.

Eventually, Maryann went to the mental hospital in Tacoma, and they got her stabilized on her medicines and placed in a group home when she was released. She has done very well in group homes and has had very good care. They give her medicine on time, and she eats on time. She is helped when they see she is building resistance to medicines and in general is well cared for. These are not institutions because she is free to leave—to go to the library, movies, shopping, or dine out. The group home does have rules, but they are for the residents' benefit. The residents receive gifts on their birthday and at Christmas, purchased from the staff budget. They can go for overnight visits, but the group home is there home. They feel very insecure if they are away from their home for very long. We tried to bring Maryann to our home when we moved back to Idaho. That didn't work very well. After a very short time, she got nervous, forgot which meds to take, and got volatile. We don't bring her down here anymore, as it sets us both up to fail. She gets lonely for us, and we try to go see her as often as we can. Her older son, Todd, and his family live in Seattle, so they see her fairly often and visit on the phone. Todd takes care of any needs she has that the home doesn't offer. He also takes her out to eat fairly often, and that helps her also.

Every day is a struggle for Maryann. The medicine has kept her fairly stable, but it has robbed her of her teeth. She has ten teeth left. The medicines are very hard on the body and the side effects are terrible, so they give meds to counteract the side effects. The medication also causes weight gain, and Maryann also developed diabetes, which they treat. She was very heavy, but she has lost a lot of weight and is only about thirty pounds over what she should be. She looks a lot healthier in that respect.

Todd is almost thirty-two and has two children, a boy and a girl. Maryann loves her grandchildren; they bring her a lot of joy. She gets excited when Todd and his family come to take her out. Her younger son is twenty-five, and he still lives with us. He is working and hopes to move back to Seattle someday soon. Maryann's children appear very healthy and show no indication of the disorders she fights daily.

We have spent hours in prayer for her, shed buckets of tears, and experienced miles of frustration before reaching a point of some kind of normal for her and for us. We also have a modicum of peace. The Lord gives us that "peace that passes all understanding," and we couldn't live very well without it. Hope is always out there, even when there seems to be no hope. Don't ever fail to lean upon God, who is our provider and the stronghold of joy in our life. He is our hope and the provider of our faith. When we lose hope and faith, we lose the will to live.

After all of these trials and testing, I took my faith one step farther and became an ordained minister. I don't pastor a church, although I do pastor a small group of people, as well as those I come in contact with along the way. It was a step for me and for however the Lord wants to use me.

As I write this book, I pray that it will minister to you as He ministered to me as I walked out this journey. I am still on the journey. I have no idea what awaits me around the bend, but I know my Lord will be with me all of the way. I also know that He is with my family, my husband, and my children, and He will minister to them in each of their needs and protect them all the way. He is a great and mighty God.

Polio: The Dreaded Disease

The Stealer of Life and Limb

hen I was in the eighth grade and my sister, Penny, was in the fourth, she became ill and was home from school for several days. She was running a temperature, and when she would get up out of bed, her head would hang to one side and she walked with a stiff gait.

My father called the doctor, and Dr. Samson came to the house—this was when doctors made house calls. He didn't take long to insist that she go to the hospital immediately, where doctors performed a spinal tap. It confirmed what Dr. Samson had suspected. Penny was diagnosed with polio. This was in the spring of 1955, a time when polio was running rampant throughout the nation and around the world. We were shocked and terrified, as well as heartsick.

My dad rode in the ambulance with Penny to California, where she was being rushed to a larger hospital that was better prepared to deal with Penny's needs. My dad was crying. I was crying too, but it really unnerved me to see him cry—I had never seen him cry before. We didn't know if Penny would live or die or be bound to an iron lung for the rest of her life. The iron lung was a device that pumped oxygen into the lungs because polio paralyzed the lungs. If not that, a polio victim's legs could be paralyzed. It was a very hard time for our family and for the many families who were facing this disease.

The polio vaccine was introduced a year after my sister became ill. The polio vaccine was discovered and developed by Dr. Salk, and he became a medical hero. Not since the invention of penicillin had there been something so marvelous. The vaccine was put into sugar cubes with a dropper, and we ate the cube. I never contracted polio. It is strange how one person would get it and no one else in the same family would get it. However, I was given an injection of a substance called gamma globulin, which was to build up my natural resistance to disease.

My sister did recover after several months in the hospital in California. When they released her to come home, she had a brace on her right arm and hand and another brace on her left leg. The disease left a trail of paralysis diagonally across her body. Her right hand is still affected although she has not had a brace since she was a child. The thumb on her right hand sits at a funny angle on her hand, but she uses that hand and that thumb anyway. She is amazing. During that time in the hospital and after she came home, she endured many torturous hours of therapy.

My father decided to take her to a tiny town called Golconda, where there were natural mineral hot springs. He believed that the water in these springs would be therapeutic and help her recover. My father was not very educated as far as book learning, but his mind was sharp, and he probably would have been a great doctor.

There were mineral pools housed in an old hotel, bar, and restaurant in Golconda. We went every other night for weeks, and our dad would get into the pool with Penny and work with her, moving all of her limbs and exercising them in the pool.

He also encouraged her to swim. She didn't think she could, but she finally attempted it and found she could swim really well. When she first started doing these exercises, it would leave an oily film on top of the water. The mineral water was drawing the impurities out of her body. After a while, this stopped. She began to move with amazing agility and soon no longer had to wear braces. By that fall, she was back in school. She still has a slight limp, which is noticeable when she is tired, but she completely recovered from what could have been debilitating for the rest of her life. This disease could have killed her or kept her captive, but what was meant for evil was turned around for good. The tears of despair have been turned into tears of joy. Praise God!

She has lived a fruitful life, has married, and has two sons, a daughter-in-law, and two young grandsons. She went back to college after her sons were in elementary school, graduated, and worked in a local hospital in medical records for twenty years.

She has never let adversity keep her from doing what she wanted and needed to do. She is a real hero in the battle of life.

Looking Back
over Time

As I look back on my own family and even farther back to my great-great-grandparents, there have been many tears and reasons for mothers and fathers to weep.

My great-grandparents Reil, left Germany in the 1880s and came to the New World to settle and raise a family. Their parents must have experienced some tortuous grief and sense of loss. To my knowledge, they never saw their children again. I am sure letters were sent, but the mail was slow, and it took a long time. I know they never saw their grandchildren or great-grandchildren. They were literally worlds apart. The fear and loss must have been horrendous.

My great-grandparents settled in California, between Duns Glenn and Paradise Valley. They eventually owned two ranches, where they had four children, one of which was my grandmother. When those children grew up, some of them moved away, another time of tears and separation.

My great-grandmother and great-grandfather on Grandpa Nelson's side were from Wales. There again, I am sure they left a trail of tears as they headed for the New World.

During World War I, my great-grandparents Nelson, lost several children. Some died in the war; some were wounded or lost limbs or their minds. How sad, and yet as I look back, my great-grandmother had faith and hope, and my great-grandfather had a great sense of humor. Even through their losses, their Lord sustained them.

My own grandfather Nelson, suffered from depression and took his own life, leaving my grandmother and their only child to face the world alone. My mom was eleven years old when her daddy died. My grandmother not only grieved the loss of her husband, but her mother-in-law accused her of murdering him. She endured that false accusation the rest of her life. Here were two mothers who had broken hearts that drove them to tears. My great-grandmother had to be out of her mind with the loss of her oldest child. My grandmother was of German descent and was often stoic in her grief. Often, she was unapproachable in her grief, and my mother mentioned that often when she returned from school, her mother would not talk to her. It had nothing to do with my mom and everything to do with my grandmother, who was trying to deal with the grief, loss, and hopelessness of being left with trying to provide for her child, as well as the cruel accusations.

She endured, she lived, she provided for her child, and she trained her last horse at the age of seventy. She had ridden horses from the time she was a little girl, and her love for horses never diminished over the years. She had a brother, who had to help out on the ranches once he was old enough, but she helped and worked outside because that was where her heart was. She trained many horses in her lifetime, and so to her, it was no big thing to train another one. Her age didn't deter her at all. Billy, the horse, turned into a fine horse, which she eventually sold. She could be very proud of her accomplishments, although I am not sure she thought so. To this granddaughter, she was a grand lady. She was strong and resourceful, and she walked through adversity with her head held high.

I am like her in many ways. She was a strong influence in my life. She was proud to be an American, as it gave her freedom to be who she was. I am proud to be an American, and I would not want to be anything else. But just like each of us, America has endured great trials and many tears. Even our enemies come here to go to school and then return to their country and try to contrive ways to destroy our nation after they were allowed to benefit from our education systems.

The nation wept in despair and disbelief over the Civil War and the death of President Lincoln. Years later, the nation wept in despair and disbelief when President Kennedy was struck down in the prime of his life. The world grieved right along with his wife, children, mother, and siblings and collective family. This was only the beginning. Then his brother, Robert Kennedy, was shot, and again, while the world was watching, causing wives and mothers around the world to weep, as did fathers, sisters, and brothers.

We, as a nation, have grieved and wept over the loss of our sons and daughters around the world in the wars around us. Young people who came home from the military either died, or lost arms and legs or their minds in the horrors of war. Mothers have the right to cry.

There are so many types of losses: the loss of movement due to injury or stroke; the loss of hair or life due to cancer or other deadly diseases; the loss of a friend, a marriage, or a pregnancy or hope.

Loss of hope and faith causes loss of a reason to live. But God is the Father of hope and faith and joy. Look to Him when life appears bleak. He is waiting for you to seek Him, so that He might comfort you and give you peace.

As you have read this journey of life, mine and others, I hope that through it all you saw or sensed God comforting, encouraging, and reaching out to the ones in need. He never let them lose hope in their grieving, always helping them to move forward. How did He do this? He used people in each of these journeys to reach out and touch someone, to hold a hand, give a hug, or make a phone call. Will you be ready to reach out to someone who is hurting, and if you are hurting, will you look to see who is reaching out to you? When you have God in your life, there is always One who is reaching out to you.

Our loved ones are "Walking' on the streets of gold, praising their Lord and receiving their reward."*

May God bless you, always.